DISCOVERING THE UNITED STATES

# New Mexico

BY K. A. HALE

Kids Core
An Imprint of Abdo Publishing
abdobooks.com

**abdobooks.com**



Printed in China.
052024
092024

THIS BOOK CONTAINS RECYCLED MATERIALS

Cover Photo: Tim Pleasant/Shutterstock Images
Interior Photos: Shutterstock Images, 4–5, 8; William Cushman/Shutterstock Images, 6; Steve Bower/Shutterstock Images, 9 (top left); Buddy Mays/Corbis/Getty Images, 9 (top right); John Silver/Shutterstock Images, 9 (bottom left); Kayla Blundell/Shutterstock Images, 9 (bottom right); Neil Lockhart/Shutterstock Images, 10; Granger Historical Picture Archive, 12–13; Dan Kaplan/Shutterstock Images, 14; Paul Ratje/AFP/Getty Images, 17; Dr. Alan Lipkin/Shutterstock Images, 18; Sean Pavone/Shutterstock Images, 20–21, 22, 28 (bottom left); Frankie Wo/Shutterstock Images, 24; Doug Meek/Shutterstock Images, 25; John A. Davis/Shutterstock Images, 26; Greg Meland/Shutterstock Images, 28 (top left); Red Line Editorial, 28 (top right), 29; Cheri Alguire/Shutterstock Images, 28 (bottom right)

Editor: Marley Richmond
Series Designer: Katharine Hale

**Library of Congress Control Number: 2023949360**

**Publisher's Cataloging-in-Publication Data**

Names: Hale, K. A., author.
Title: New Mexico / by K. A. Hale
Description: Minneapolis, Minnesota: Abdo Publishing, 2025 | Series: Discovering the United States | Includes online resources and index.
Identifiers: ISBN 9781098294014 (lib. bdg.) | ISBN 9798384913283 (ebook)
Subjects: LCSH: U.S. states--Juvenile literature. | New Mexico--History--Juvenile literature. | Southwestern States--Juvenile literature. | Physical geography--United States--Juvenile literature.
Classification: DDC 973--dc23

All population data taken from:
"Estimates of Population by Sex, Race, and Hispanic Origin: April 1, 2020 to July 1, 2022." *US Census Bureau, Population Division*, June 2023, census.gov.

# CONTENTS

Balloon Fiesta is one of the most photographed events in the world.

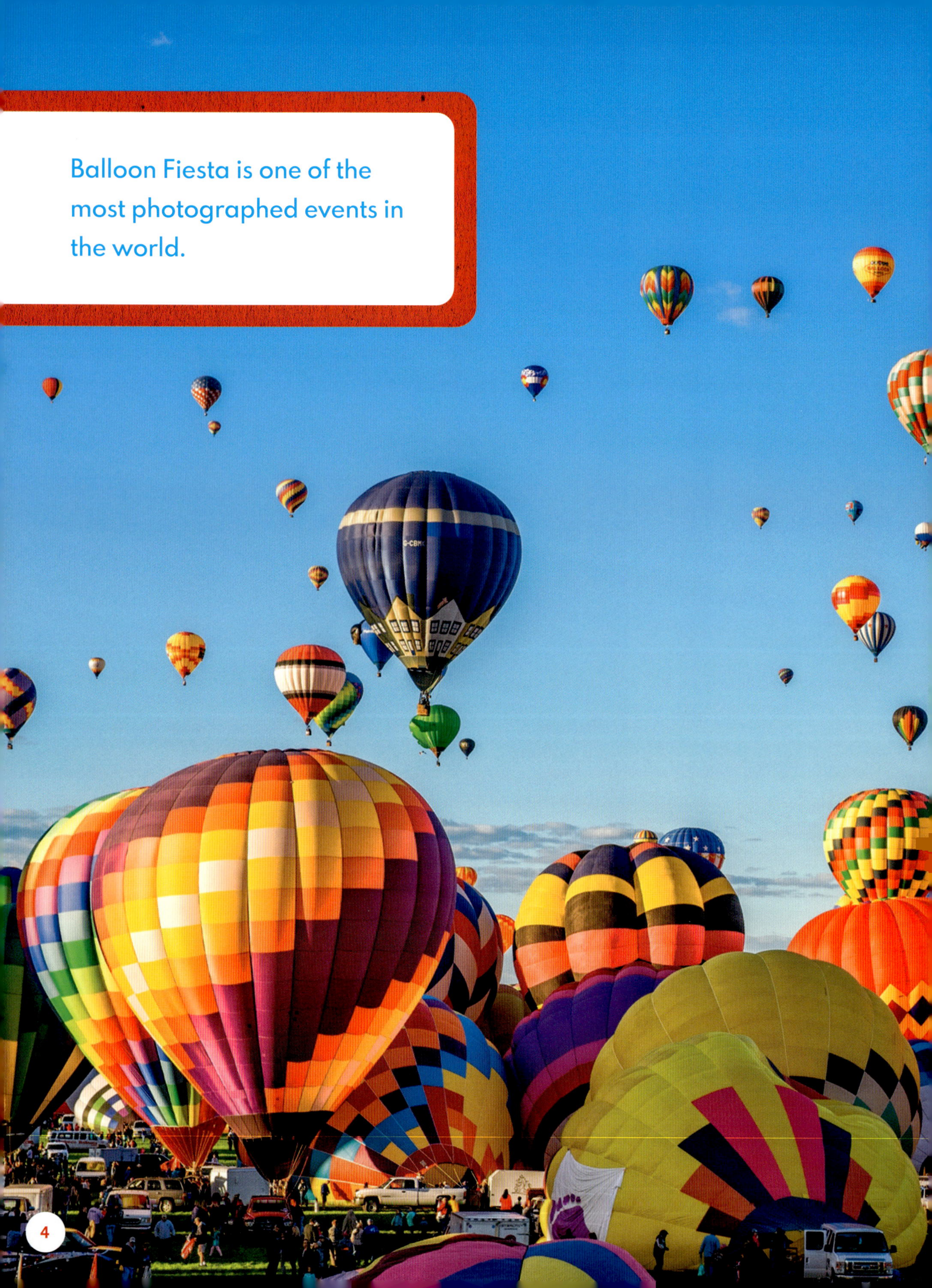

CHAPTER 1

# Flying High

It was 1972. A radio station in Albuquerque, New Mexico, was planning a celebration. The station asked Sid Cutter to help. Cutter was a local hot-air balloon pilot. He quickly organized a hot-air balloon race.

Hot-air balloon pilots can participate in many events as part of Balloon Fiesta. During Balloon Glows, pilots inflate and light up their balloons without flying.

Thirteen pilots launched from a mall parking lot. Albuquerque's Balloon Fiesta was born.

This event has grown into a beloved New Mexico tradition. The Albuquerque International Balloon Fiesta is the largest hot-air balloon event in the world. Hundreds of thousands of people come each year. They watch hundreds of balloons from all over the world take flight.

## Albuquerque Conditions

Albuquerque's low **humidity** and high **altitude** are part of what makes the city so popular for balloonists. The wind blows one direction at lower altitude. It blows the opposite direction at higher altitude. Balloon pilots can fly one direction. Then they can fly higher and float back toward where they started.

New Mexico's state flag shows a red sun symbol. The design is inspired by an ancient symbol from Zia Pueblo.

## The Land of Enchantment

New Mexico is in the West region of the United States. Arizona is west of the state. Colorado borders New Mexico to the north. Oklahoma lies to the east. Texas is to the east and south. Mexico lies to the south.

New Mexico's beautiful landscapes have earned it the nickname the Land of Enchantment. Most of the state's land rises more

# New Mexico Facts

**DATE OF STATEHOOD**
January 6, 1912

**CAPITAL**
Santa Fe

**POPULATION**
2,113,344

**AREA**
121,590 square miles (314,917 sq km)

**STATE BIRD**

Greater roadrunner

**STATE TREE**

Piñon pine

**STATE FLOWER**

Yucca

**STATE COOKIE**

Biscochito

Each US state has a different population, size, and capital city. States also have state symbols.

than 4,000 feet (1,220 m) above sea level. This is considered a very high **altitude**. There are many mountain ranges in the state, such as the Sangre de Cristo mountains.

New Mexico's deserts are home to many interesting rock formations. Church Rock stands in Red Rock Park.

More than 4,500 species of plants and animals are found in New Mexico. They are adapted to the hot, dry climate. Juniper, cottonwood, and pine trees are common in the state. Lizards and snakes roam the deserts. Coyotes and mountain lions prowl for prey.

## New Mexico's Climate

New Mexico has lots of sunshine. It has little rain or snow. Summers are hot and dry. Winters are usually mild. Mountain areas are colder and get more snow. Forests are common in the mountains. Plains and deserts cover the flatter parts of the state.

### Further Evidence

Look at the website below. Does it give any new evidence to support Chapter One?

#### How Does a Hot-Air Balloon Fly?

abdocorelibrary.com/discovering-new-mexico

The Zuni people are related to the Ancestral Pueblo peoples. The Zuni are known for their artwork.

CHAPTER 2

# The People of New Mexico

American Indians have lived in what is now New Mexico for about 13,000 years. Two early peoples in the state were the Ancestral Pueblo and Mogollon cultures. By the 1500s, Diné (or Navajo) and Apache peoples also lived in New Mexico.

The Taos people built Taos Pueblo before Spanish explorers arrived in New Mexico. People have lived there for about 1,000 years.

Spanish explorers came to New Mexico in the mid-1500s. They called American Indian communities pueblos. There were about 100 pueblos at that time.

In 1598, Spanish **settlers** created a **colony** in New Mexico. The settlers forced American

Indians to work for them. In 1680, many pueblos joined together. They forced the Spanish out of New Mexico. Colonists returned 12 years later. But they agreed to stop forced labor.

New Mexico was a part of Spain until 1821. Then it became part of Mexico when the country gained independence from Spain. New Mexico eventually became a US state in 1912.

Today, about 50 percent of New Mexico's population is Hispanic or Latino. There are 23 federally recognized American Indian tribes in New Mexico. About 11 percent of New Mexicans are American Indian. White people make up 35.7 percent of the population. About 2.7 percent are Black, and 2 percent are Asian.

# Culture

New Mexico's culture has strong Spanish and American Indian influences. Adobe architecture is common throughout the state. Adobe bricks are made from mud and straw. Flat roofs are common in this style. Long beams support them.

Pueblo and Mexican food has inspired New Mexican **cuisine**. Common ingredients are

## Dance in New Mexico

There are many dance traditions in New Mexico. Ballet folklórico is a form of traditional Mexican dancing. Dancers swirl large skirts covered in colorful ribbons. Flamenco is a dance style from Spain. Albuquerque is the flamenco capital of North America.

Dancing is one way New Mexicans connect to their culture. People dance ballet folklórico as part of a Cinco de Mayo festival in Mesilla, New Mexico.

blue corn and beans. Sopaipillas are made of fried dough. They can be stuffed, drizzled with honey, or eaten plain. Red and green chiles are made into sauces and toppings. *Carne adovada* is a New Mexican pork dish cooked with red chiles. Biscochito cookies come from Spain. They are light and buttery.

Hatch, New Mexico, is known as the chile capital of the world.

# Economy

Farming and ranching are important industries in New Mexico. Sheep and cattle are raised in the state. New Mexico farmers produce more than 120,000 tons (108,900 metric tons) of chiles each year. **Natural resources** are also important to the state's economy. These include oil and natural gas. The state also makes renewable energy from solar and wind power.

New Mexico is home to important military and research sites. These include Los Alamos and Sandia National Laboratories. They provide jobs for many New Mexicans.

## Explore Online

Visit the website below. Does it give any new information that wasn't in Chapter Two?

### Adobe Brick

abdocorelibrary.com/discovering-new-mexico

Old Town is a cultural center of Albuquerque, New Mexico.

CHAPTER 3

# Places in New Mexico

New Mexico has lots of exciting places to visit. Albuquerque is the largest city in the state. Its historic Old Town is home to shops and museums. People can buy handmade jewelry and crafts from local artists.

Santa Fe is the oldest capital city in the United States.

The National Hispanic Cultural Center is in Albuquerque. So is the Indian Pueblo Cultural Center.

Santa Fe is New Mexico's capital city. The Palace of the Governors there is the oldest continuously used public building in the country.

Visitors can enjoy the city's museums, shops, and restaurants. El Rancho de las Golondrinas is a living history museum in Santa Fe. It features buildings from different periods in New Mexico's history. Volunteers wear historical clothing. They teach visitors about the state's history.

Taos is a city known for art. Art galleries and museums are found throughout Taos.

### Roswell

In 1947, a strange object crashed in Roswell, New Mexico. The military said it was a weather balloon. But many people thought it was a flying saucer. Today, Roswell is home to the Unidentified Flying Object (UFO) Festival. The International UFO Museum is there too. Buildings and signs in town are decorated with aliens.

Even in the middle of summer, the dunes at White Sands National Park don't get hot like a beach would. That is because gypsum does not hold heat the same way other sand does.

Just outside of the city is the Taos Pueblo. This is the oldest continually inhabited community in the United States.

## Natural Beauty

New Mexico is home to many natural wonders. The state has two national parks. White Sands

Visitors can walk along the Big Room Trail in Carlsbad Caverns. This path is 1.25 miles (2 km) long.

is the world's largest field of gypsum dunes. Gypsum is a **mineral**. Carlsbad Caverns has about 119 caves with limestone formations. Visitors can learn more about New Mexico's history at the state's 14 national monuments.

El Malpais National Monument is one of New Mexico's Dark Sky sites.

New Mexico has eight Dark Sky areas. These areas are protected for stargazing.

In New Mexico, people can watch hot-air balloons soar across the sky. They can try traditional food made with chiles. Lovers of art, history, nature, and more can find something to enjoy in New Mexico.

# Primary Source

New Mexico government official Jen Paul Schroer spoke about the state. She said:

> It's easy to feel proud of what we have here in New Mexico. . . . The things that make us proud to be New Mexicans are the destinations that combine the adventure and the **authenticity** of the Land of Enchantment.

Source: Jen Paul Schroer. "PSA 'Let's Save What Makes NM True.'" *YouTube*, uploaded by VisitNewMexico, 29 Jan. 2021, youtube.com. Accessed 15 Jan. 2024.

## Point of View

What is the author's point of view on this topic? What is your point of view? Write a short essay about how they are similar and different.

# State Map

Rio Grande River

**KEY**

- Capital
- Park
- City or town
- Point of interest

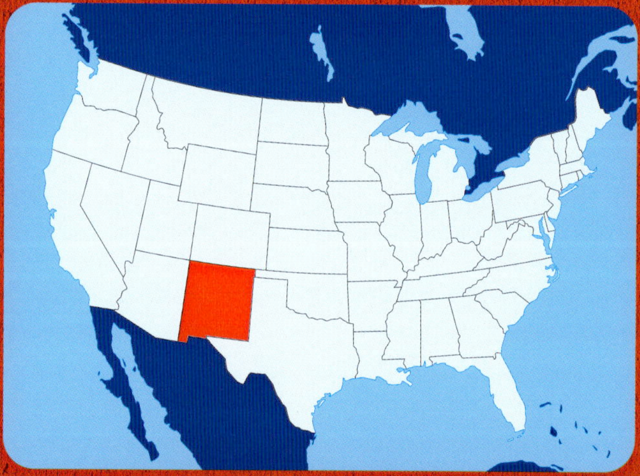

Santa Fe

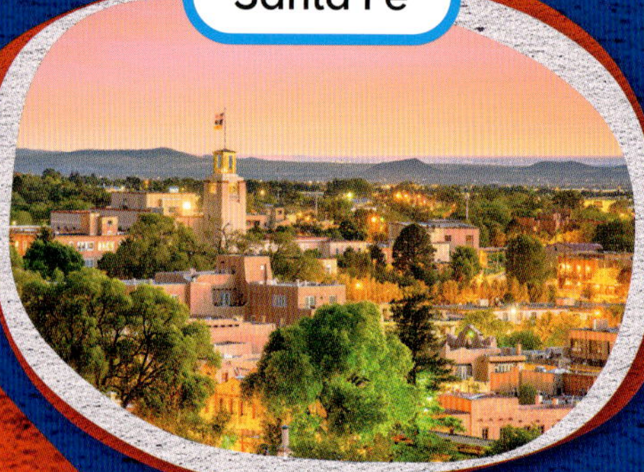

Roswell

# New Mexico: The Land of Enchantment

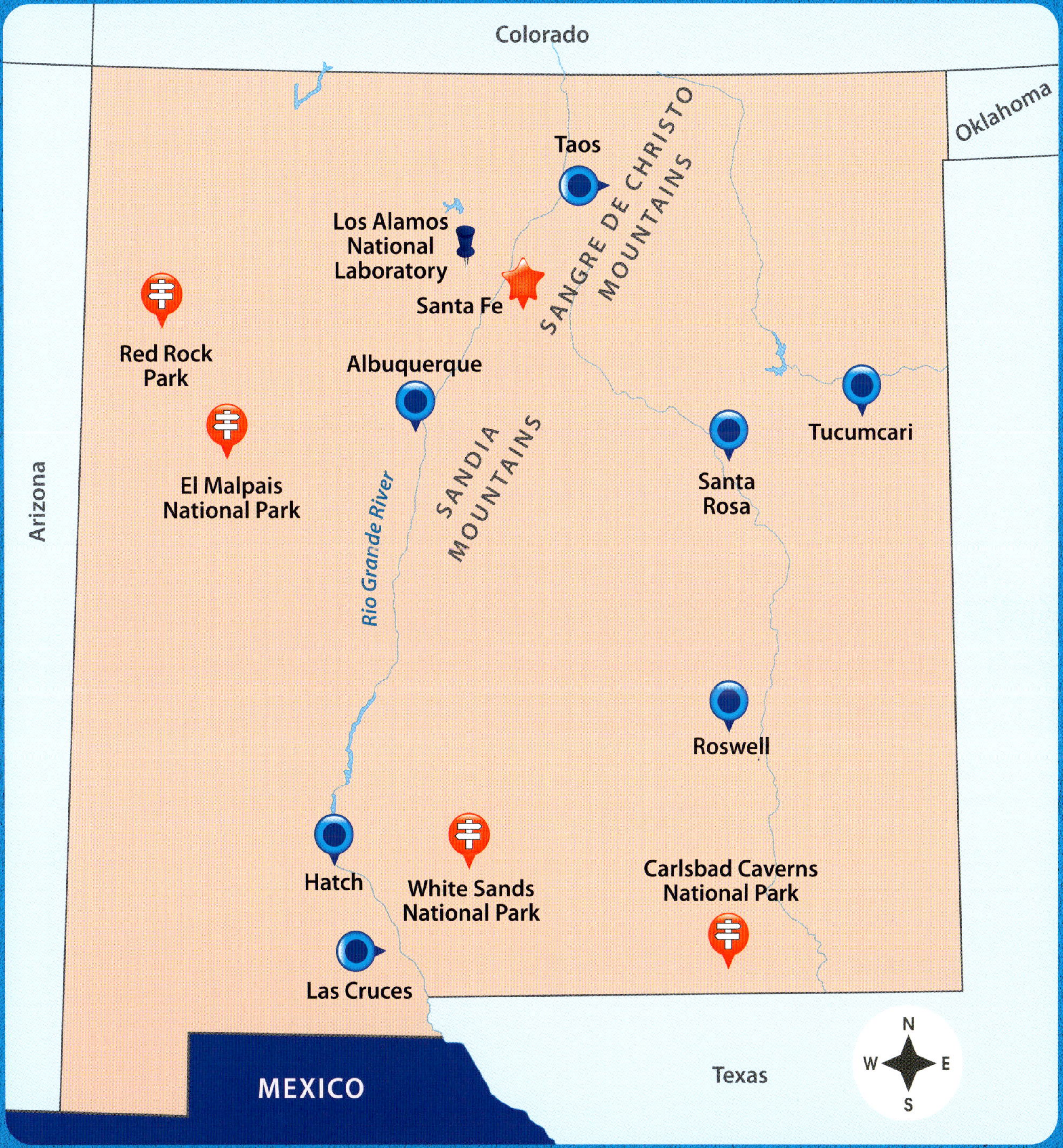

# Glossary

**altitude**
height above sea level

**authenticity**
the quality of being real and original

**colony**
an area that is controlled by another country

**cuisine**
a style of cooking

**humidity**
the amount of moisture in air

**mineral**
a substance formed in the earth that is not of an animal or a plant

**natural resources**
materials found in nature that can be used by people

**settlers**
people who moved to a new area

# Online Resources

To learn more about New Mexico, visit our free resource websites below.

Core Library CONNECTION
FREE! COMMON CORE MULTIMEDIA RESOURCES

Visit **abdocorelibrary.com** or scan this QR code for free Common Core resources for teachers and students, including vetted activities, multimedia, and booklinks, for deeper subject comprehension.

Booklinks NONFICTION NETWORK
FREE! ONLINE NONFICTION RESOURCES

Visit **abdobooklinks.com** or scan this QR code for free additional online weblinks for further learning. These links are routinely monitored and updated to provide the most current information available.

# Learn More

Aspen Song Kids. *The Sacred Spiral.* Nighthawk, 2023.

Burgan, Michael. *Albuquerque.* Arcadia, 2022.

Murray, Julie. *New Mexico.* Abdo, 2020.

# Index



# About the Author

K. A. Hale spent her childhood in Albuquerque and misses the Sandia Mountains every day. She was lucky enough to travel to New Mexico right before writing this book, and she got to fly at the Balloon Fiesta. She now lives in Minnesota, where she writes, edits, and designs children's books.